BRENT MACLAINE
PROMETHEUS RECONSIDERS FIRE

The Acorn Press
Charlottetown
2016

© 2016 by Brent MacLaine

All rights reserved. No part of this publication may be reproduced, stored in a retrieval system, or transmitted, in any form or by any means, without the prior written permission of the publisher or, in case of photocopying or other reprographic copying, a licence from the Canadian Copyright Licensing Agency.

ACORNPRESS

P.O. Box 22024
Charlottetown, Prince Edward Island
C1A 9J2
acornpresscanada.com

Edited by Dr. Anne Compton
Design by Matt Reid
Printed in Canada

Library and Archives Canada
Cataloguing in Publication

MacLaine, Brent, author
Prometheus reconsiders fire / Brent MacLaine.

Poems.
Issued in print and electronic formats.
ISBN 978-1-927502-63-1 (paperback).--ISBN 978-1-927502-64-8 (html)

I. Title.

| PS8575.L323P76 2016 | C811'.6 | C2016-901269-7 |
| | | C2016-901270-0 |

Funded by the Government of Canada | Canada | Canada Council for the Arts   Conseil des Arts du Canada

We acknowledge the [financial] support of the Government of Canada, the Canada Council for the Arts and the Province of Prince Edward Island.

for Kay

Also by Brent MacLaine

Wind and Root (Véhicule)
These Fields Were Rivers (Goose Lane)
Shades of Green (Acorn)
Athena Becomes a Swallow (Goose Lane)
Landmarks: An Anthology of New Atlantic Canadian Poetry of the Land. Ed. with Hugh MacDonald (Acorn)

CONTENTS

The Northern Flicker 2
Prometheus Reconsiders Fire 3

*

The North River Fire Hall Suite I

Prologue: Ode to Sign Person 7
Gratitude is the sign of a noble soul 8
A spark neglected makes a mighty fire 10
The speedway ends at the cemetery 12
Chance takers are accident makers 14
Fire takes no holiday 16
Carelessness does not bounce; it shatters 20
Happy 40th Arnold and Bernice 22

*

De Maisonneuve and Greene 25
Prochain Station: Green Line 26
A Concert at Chapelle Notre-Dame-de-Bon-Secours 27
Highrise View Early Morning 29
Stargazing 30
Columbus and 67th Street 31
City Park in June 32

*

Doors 34
No Scissors on Sunday 35
Sestina for Early Morning at the Service Station Coffee Shop 36
The Studio Boy's Private View 38
Night Vision on a Road Trip 39
Early Morning Mist 40
Not One Thing 41
Once in a Lifetime 42
Provisional 43

*

Queen Anne's Lace 45
Bestiary 46
Webworm 47
Paradisaea apoda **48**
For the Humpback Whales 50
Lake Massawipi 54
Drift 55

*

The Brazen Bull 57
The Dictator's Son 58
Lone Wolf 60
Flowers by the Gates 61
Elegy for Mikhail Kalashnikov 62
Baumgartner's Fall 63
Lost with *The Titanic*: An Inventory 65
An Architect Visits the Sick 69

*

The North River Fire Hall Suite II

The worst fire escape plan is no plan 72
Short-cuts in life cut life short 74
Firefighters save hearts and homes 76
Always leave yourself an emergency exit 78
Luck runs out, but safety is good for life 80

*

Relics 83

*

Notes and Acknowledgements 88

All things, O priests, are on fire.

– "The Fire Sermon," from *The Mahavagga*,

The Northern Flicker

Sun-up – and your arrival from the east
over the evergreens and barley field
announces something new, something just released
upon the day, an invocation revealed
by the fiery gold flaring from your wings –
yet one more beginning on the plush lawn,
what your song and feathered flurry brings
to the false spirea which you light upon.
As for the splotch of redness on your cheek –
that would be memory's mark of immolation,
the sign that every burning must bespeak
a promise in the ash of what's undone.
Thus, wary of death and with watchful eye,
you peck the earth eager for life – then fly.

Prometheus Reconsiders Fire

Prometheus calls me on.
Prometheus calls me: Son,
We'll both go off together
In this delightful weather.

– Patrick Kavanagh, "The Self-slaved"

At least there's a view. A promontory trumps
an inland quarry. One gets a sense of scale,
one's positioning in the reach of speechless things.
Here comes the dawn dragging a coastal cloud
across horizon's sky, a tattered one
like a great red wing with many feathers,
reminder – as though I needed it – of what's to come,
of what I'm up against, of consequences,
and the scope of my misdeed. Daily, the crimson
spreads a show of sovereignty, a lingering rebuke.
Vainly, I kick the rubble stones at my feet
and send them tumbling seaward down the cliff.

The beauty of it caught my eye – such colour
dancing in the hearth, such warmth, such power
from cauldron planets flaming through the sky.
What harm in offering one small portion
to ease the days and nights of my creation –
a lamp for darkness, a flame for roasting meat?
All this from a glowing coal I hid within
a fennel stalk – my flower blossoming with fire.
Regret? Not when darkness falls and I see
the hovel windows lit along the forest edge
all down the coast – their flickering, however dim,
lets me know, we share the signalling of stars.

Rock and flesh – is that the story here?
The dumb crumbling of time layer by layer
and always the body's nervy watch for pain.
Foresight? The suffering one could expect –
the dreaded bird arriving, starved and crude –
but who could know the dread of his predictable
return, the jab of his appointments, the daily
repetitions like the sea itself, wave devouring wave,
tide after tide, unknowing and indifferent.
This ceaseless cycling of the hurting and the healing –
one grows doubtful of its end – of any end –
sidelined here in a scrappy corner of the Caucasus.

As for release, I've done with rage, choose not
to compete with canyon winds and thunder-wrath;
instead, my unflinching, self-shaped quietude,
I'm proud to say, will be my call to generations –
though I admit, the future and its purpose
become a dying whisper in the trees.
Still, today a boat sailed by, at a leeward lean,
bobbing beneath its dirty puffed out sail,
heading for the far shore. It was comical.
But I did – heedless of the chafing – I did
shake my ankle chains. I might as well, I thought,
make my bruising knell like chimes upon the wind.

THE NORTH RIVER
FIRE HALL SUITE I

Prologue

Ode to Sign Person

Speak to me, sing to me, Sign Person,
with coal-black lettering on caution yellow.
Guide me on my daily commute past the gas bars,
convenience stores, and fast-food restaurants.
Admonish me for my neglect;
inspire me with adage and epigram
that I may rest my work soul in an uncomplaining place.
Comfort me with drive-by wisdom
from the *Book of Quotes*.
Keep me responsibly informed of fund-raisers
for the Bantam Bulldogs and municipal meetings
to debate rezoning of Mackenzie's farm.
Forgive my failure to devise a foolproof fire escape plan,
and may Google Scripture make me
judicious, tolerant, and reasonable at all times.
I praise you, you who make the weekly changes
and mark the seasons with seasonal wishes,
you who write the roadside manual for motorists
in need of sober counselling and sound advice –
your sign, a frontispiece for cheerfulness, rescue, and relief.

GRATITUDE IS THE SIGN OF A NOBLE SOUL.

I

That sounds like you –
whose level eye could always find
small mercies in the August garden:
the sweet-swollen root and fat-podded peas,
nourishment for long winter nights
when there was time to savour
providence and richly gravied stews
simmering atop the kitchen stove.
A sated appetite meant that you
could contemplate your miseries:
storm-lifted shingles, combustible hay
in the high loft that spread its fiery loss,
miscarried calves, infections,
early deaths, and a mouthful of life's lacerations.
Still – after solitude upon a night wind,
there was butter-crusted bread,
well-roasted meat, and blood-red preserves
that helped you keep your colour
when beyond the steamed-up windows
shocking drifts of snow blanched the yard.
You were wise to bank the drafty sills
with shale, staunch the flow of sharp winds
leaking in, and stall the creep of frost
up the lean of floral-papered walls.

A SPARK NEGLECTED MAKES A MIGHTY FIRE.

II

– which explains why neighbours gathered
round the charred farmhouse beams
smouldering in the cellar pit two days later.
They shook their heads and looked out to sea
for restitution – for explanations that fell away
with the falling tide. Bits of blistered furniture
lay by the stable door, salvaged kitchen ornaments,
three enamelled pots, and a yellow bowl.
The Clydesdale mare stomped her heavy feet,
and strange fleshy smells settled down
like a fouled fog among the panicked weeds.
Flue-fire, ash-bin coals quickened by a wind,
toppled lamp, or lightning strike – it scarcely mattered,
what with sun-cracked shingles, dusty straw,
and so much well-seasoned wood.
Firecracker firs and torch-dry pines
stood around as tinder for all their lives.
Smoke they understood as loss,
something dark from what had used them up,
something votive, an offering to carry it away.

THE SPEEDWAY ENDS AT THE CEMETERY.

III

– which doesn't mean risking it all
in one grand Daytona moment,
nicking a red fender in the S-curve,
or a slow-motion swerve into a smoking
turn-around, or one final spectacular
triple roll over the barricade,
front wheel de-axled and spinning
a rainbow arc over the gasping crowd.

No, not that, nor even the truncated
shoulder-check during a slushy lane change
on your way to an early morning meeting
of The Board. Such manoeuvring
through the radar trap of the daily commute
warrants priestly absolution but hardly
sweet inscriptions gouged on granite
overlooking freshly tamped sod.

Nor, for that matter, your childhood
bicycle dash down the dusty path
to the road-end, past the crowd of alders
and the ghoulish goldenrod – warp drive
on that route ends with the low tide of memory:
shorebirds pecking at their own reflections,
sandbars underfoot, beached strings of kelp,
and sea-worn stones waiting to be moved.

It scarcely matters. Rubber tires
rolling down the well-waxed corridors
is speed enough on the way to lunch –
creamed carrots and a baked fish –
and afterwards, to the terrace where one
can overlook the potted palms, the sloping hill,
and that grove of poplars bunched like rows
of markers in a weedy, unmowed field.

CHANCE TAKERS ARE ACCIDENT MAKERS.

IV

– but what are the odds?
Backing Fortune's Buddy, for example,
just because his glossy brown flanks
remind you of the chestnuts underneath
the backyard tree that September
when you noticed, for the first time,
something lithe in the way things happened –
weather on its way out wheeled round
and swamped the late-returning lobster boat;
the weed-covered plank over the unused well
dissolved in subtle rot; and sly, nocturnal flames
were too much for wet potato sacks
slapped against the gable end.
Quick Thinking or Double Beams
or Two Coats of Paint were losers
by a quarter mile. Numbers and Prayers
fell aside. And yet, placing a perfecta bet
seemed the prudent choice, even when we knew
that Buddy often broke gait as he stumbled down the home stretch.

FIRE TAKES NO HOLIDAY.

V

But if it did, where would it go?
Somewhere cold and wet, I suppose –
in November to the foggy coast of Oregon,
fizzling on a damp log beneath some dripping fronds.

Clearly, fire works hard –
flint spark and lightning strike,
long hours and overtime, from fire-pit on,
its duties are extensive:

Forger –
smith of the wrought shield, weaponry,
plow, blackened tools, hinges for the world's openings and closings,
and horseshoes for travelling continents.
Crucible of peoples.

Destroyer –
of fortress and forest, the flaming arrow,
Vulcan blast, and lava licking
at the cottage doorstep, edging closer
to the kindling of daily breath.

Lamplighter –
ale-hall rush and candle in sconce,
beacon to wanderers at sea,
wick-glow on the kitchen table for school books
and mending the torn shirt.

Purifier –
of failures, scrap-heap rubble,
torn and broken things, splintered boards,
remnants of remnants, cast-off branches,
infected shroud, and all unusables.

Kitchen labourer –
stove warmth, yeast starter,
firebox oven heat for risen bread;
torch of twisted paper to singe the plucked bird,
and coal glow for toasting delectables.

Matchmaker –
bonfire beneath an approving moon
for shore-side lovers on a windless summer night
stirring sparks that drop and hiss
upon the full tide that falls and falls and falls.

CARELESSNESS DOES NOT BOUNCE; IT SHATTERS.

VI

But if it did – would we take advantage
of the micro-moments of reprieve,
the second chance for a swift re-do?
Or would we mourn the loss of all things gone awry?
The heartbeat gasp as the soapy
blue-willow plate falls onto the kitchen tiles;
the butcher blade tumbling with a knife-thrower's
spin directly at your foot; the snarling skill-saw
lunging from its two-by-four at your throat.
What about anticipation, horror, and regret?
In the paradise of no-disasters,
the ditch-bound car flies balletically,
lands upright tap- tap- taptaptap-ing
on a mat of soft green lawn. Oil-spills
become a wholesome rain, each drop
a rainbow prism in the post-storm sun.
And those backstreet explosions?
The ill-timed fuse that heaves
the bricks and shrapnel skyward,
pocks the clouds, and then becomes
a child's delight spreading celebration
everywhere – a screaming melody over
the beat of a deep percussive bass.
Follow the bouncing ball.

HAPPY 40TH ANNIVERSARY ARNOLD AND BERNICE

VII

"... and many happy returns" –
all along the receiving line.
Men in checkered shirts joke with Arnold:
"You're good for forty more."

Bernice's corsage has collapsed a bit,
and Arnold's over-sized boutonniere
takes up most of his best suit's lapel.
In the Sears portrait on display, the blues
and burgundies are a touch over-exposed.
Bernice looks flushed; Arnold, sour.

Next to the punch bowl, rows of sandwiches –
egg salad, tuna, minced ham – sit neatly
trimmed beside the filigree of pastel sweets –
strawberry tarts, lemon squares, and coconut balls.

We know little of their private lives,
unwrapped desires, couplings after arguments,
moods late at night, or who they are
when all alone in empty rooms – yet
their being here among us all these years
is a sign of something built: something
more than fences in good repair,
a well-weeded garden, fattened yearlings,
and fresh coats of paint on house and barn,
something more than keeping up the place
and putting on a good spread.

It's the way they sit shoulder to shoulder,
a well-pressed dignity, but entirely unaware
of what they have achieved. For sure,
it warrants celebration on a Fire Hall sign –
it's something every Trans-Canada motorist
should know about when driving by.

In town, leaves were paper, but the hills were a flock of faiths;
To a boy who walked all day, each leaf was a green breath
Rebuilding a love I thought was dead as nails,
Blessing the death and the baptism of fire.

– Derek Walcott, "A City's Death by Fire"

De Maisonneuve and Greene

At the intersection of this and that,
the crosswalk light counts down
over and over again.
A late pedestrian makes a run for it –
his route, one of many passages timed by the second.
Some go kitty-corner to the bank, others to the *dépanneur*,
while under the hardware of the day – utility poles
and a snarl of sagging wires –
people clutching purses and packages
criss-cross to their destinations,
every purpose a secret in the summer air.
Terrace diners appraise the strength of their cappuccinos
and the flakiness of croissants,
while underneath the tables, sparrows forage for crumbs,
make several passes, then flit here and there.
On her way to the ATM, the straw-hatted lady
overtakes the homeless man who stops –
then retraces his steps, as though she reminded him
of a path he took long ago, one through a field perhaps.
Underneath the sidewalk trees that sway above it all,
cyclists weave their way with a forward lean.
A terrier strains his leash, and the heart
of the Portuguese water dog breaks by the fountain,
whose sunlit spray tosses up a patterning
that disappears as quickly as it shows.
Tangled in such trajectories, no one seems to notice
the warp of trees and weft of clouds –
nor the wrap of mist falling from the mountain.

Prochain Station: **Green Line**

Below the streets and offices, the travellers
lug their days into dark tunnels,
their fixed faces rebuking every cheerful ad.

So many hands clinging to the chrome bars –
texters, swipers, game-players, readers
(*The Chronicles of Something or Other*) –

past the bursts of blue light, streaks of red,
and Munch reflections, past the sooty walls,
consigned to a ride on time's high-voltage rail.

Coming or going with bags of miracle goods –
a wand of baguette, a surprise-sale shirt – they dress down
for the occasion: denim, soiled shoes, and fashion gone awry.

What is passing here cannot be captured on a screen;
ear-buds block the screech of brakes – these are miners
with hope for a headlamp aimed in front of them
quarrying ahead to their destinations.

A Concert at Chapelle Notre-Dame-de-Bon-Secours

"I prevailed on a few people to gather stone and M. de Maisonneuve had some wood cut for the framework and he helped them drag it from the woods."
– Marguerite Bourgeoys

Our walk is cold
from Champs de Mars Metro station
to Chapelle Notre-Dame-de-Bon-Secours,
and the cobbled bricks, slick with ice, slow us down.
But we have time –
time to be on time,
time to lean against the wind,
and time to share remarks on well-lit window art.

Dressed in our winter blacks,
you in your Zhivago hat,
me in my coiled red scarf,
we step arm and arm like refugees
heading to our sanctuary.
Snow lays its splotches on the grey stones of Old Montreal.

Seated at a restaurant window table,
lovers smile at us and sip champagne with Malpeque oysters.
Their waiter serves them bread.

The pews are hard tonight,
but the light from the hanging lamps shaped like ships
is soft and warm. Time past,
sailors here would have soothed their salt-cracked hands
amid the cool smiles and blue cloaks of comforting nuns.
This evening, the pianist floats her notes
easefully upon the air while the horn and violin
lift them upwards past the Mater Dei
to the rooftop where the Star of the Sea angel
winnows them with her wings.

In the sweetness of the new year,
she will see the first ship break its way to port,
splinter through crystals of St. Lawrence River ice.
Officials will bestow upon its captain The Gold-Headed Cane.
His cargo? Raw sugar from Brazil.

Highrise View Early Morning

Nothing moving yet but wisps of steam from rooftop vents.
Something must be breathing within – some kind of lung.
Sunrise clouds stretch themselves, swipe the stacks of steel,
while morning mirrors itself in squares of glass.
Aluminum, rivet, and brace, troughs and pipes
coming and going, tracking up and down the easiest routes –
something is being built; some purpose is at hand.
Red logos blister the high concrete – MANULIFE.
Yet, chased by its own shadows, a fire escape
hurries down the sooty brick, irregular and confused
over faded names: C. R.   W   Linds   H me   urniture.
Nothing is complete.

Far below, cars bead themselves around corners,
and as the sun comes more direct,
delivery vans dock at bays unloading the day's cargo.
Window shades go up, curtains part, some pinched, others torn.
Pedestrians walk perimeters, then disappear inside –
something angular and precise is beginning.
Things are beginning to intersect
beside three trees, a café bench, and one dead green spire.

What filigrees there are –
some balustrades, and cornices, a rattled arch –
announce their irony among the gridwork.
Light and movement have conspired in this;
they are mute – tell no story of what has happened here
and even less of what's to come.

A lone gull arrives from the mountain, circling,
spreading its accomplished wings.

Stargazing

The highrises loom tonight like spot-lit monuments,
while below them streetlights arch their stems,
heavy with pale blooms.

Under their blossoming, headlights and taillights
launch their colours through the dim tunnels,
tracers up and down the streets.

And the stars? Under such conditions,
according to those in the know,
the stars are best viewed from a freshly dug grave –
the mounds of sod on either side
deflecting lesser light.

Apparently, deepening one's placement in the earth
means seeing further afield –
finding purer light.

Columbus and 67th Street

The young man with ear phones cannot hear
the café's mellow music –
"Dream, dream, dream" reprised,
and not much for cantatas, the laptop crowd
inhabit silent, odourless rooms.

The coffee tastes of street,
but the customers are unaware of intersections –
that lithe lady in sandals, for example,
embracing a vase of roses –
never again will she cross paths
with the jogger leashed to his Russian hound.
Nevertheless, the point of their near collision
could be graphed with that of others:
the elderly couple holding hands,
the workers laying pipe, the grocer tidying
his rows of mangoes from Brazil.
There are unmapped constellations here,
lines to be drawn between the city's nodes,
some strange animal for the Zodiac, as yet unnamed.

The perpendiculars, too, can be accounted for –
entering and exiting the conduits of the streets,
in and out of private rooms, shops, interiors.
Behind the curtained windows and dead-bolt doors,
there are alignments of unruly children
and shambled voices; they leave messy configurations
when they dodge the sidewalk obstacles.

The rooftop greenery and potted plants blur nothing,
and the oldest brickwork, its corners rounded
by the weather, retains its patterned past.

Meanwhile, black sedans and over-ripened yellow cabs
manoeuver their way downtown,
jostling for a lifeline in the avenues.

City Park in June

Minders straighten a crooked queue of children.
"No, Bess, you have to stay with us."
Frankie, who is overcome by light and colour,
offers up a gathering of flaring dandelions,

while geese silently patrol the pond
guiding their goslings among reeds and irises,
gliding over their unease,
wary of the aging jogger breathing hard on the asphalt trail.

Although the cyclists in slick helmets
are sure of their way, the tulips – their stripes
undone – concede: they have already crashed
on the bed of last year's compacted leaves.

Couples keep to the paths, airing their secrets,
while lawnmowers choke and groan on new growth.
Old winter, who is homeless, insists on a collocation,
hangs around bleaching the park benches.

True, the juniper has spread at least another inch,
and the landscape crew is turning over sod;
nevertheless, the playground grass has lost its hold
and the numbers on the shuffleboard grow faint.

We build and we destroy, and much of what
Grows in delight and tallness will soon burn,
Accepting the terminal flame as a transformation.

– John Fuller, "Stove and Wheelbarrow"

Doors

Passage through the doors of that old gabled
house was never easy – they hung at awkward
unobliging angles, made us shoulder them.

Every entry pushed the limits of its frame,
and every exit was a tug and scrape
against a wayward warp or buckled sill.

We never saw the core of them – decades
of shellac and paint on each panelled cross –
no matter how much sanding down we did.

Rusted doorknobs rattled loose, detached,
and slouched delinquently. Screw nails stripped
their threads, went missing; hinges slid aside

their best positioning, slipped their fastenings.
To stay the January draughts leaking in
below, we rolled up the dusty kitchen throw.

Mismatched keys wobbling out of place? We tossed
them in the empty cracker tin. The rare locking?
A kitchen knife stabbed between the door and jamb.

Yet, the pocked and dented panels did their work:
marked our coming and our going, became
a portal to our larger world, and gate
to shut it out when it was best to stay within.

No Scissors on Sunday
for Marian Bruce

- Because snipping is close to clacking, and machinery speech is noise, not praise.
- Because too many openings and closings, finger and thumb, tax the hand's musculature – too much tendon work.
- Because there must be no halving or quartering on the day of wholeness – nothing riven. Enough of that on the cut-up mid-week days.
- Because, in spite of shearing cloth for hours in dim sewing-table light – shoulder cramp and neck crick – just beneath the back-stitched seams of time, tatters lurk.
- Because of all the shorn hair fallen to the kitchen floor – instrument of too much self-regard and pride.
- Because of rust.
- Because of dullness, snagging, and all threats to a smooth subdivide.
- Because of pointedness; sharp words, as caution knows, we must distrust.
- Because of punctures, a stabber in a pinch – stiletto of revenge, derangement, and despair.
- Because such gadgetry for busyness is forged in devil's fire.
- Because too much clever handiwork distracts the mind – a dubious, unholy affair.
- Because who would sever household peace? Cries of mishap and calamity fashion a discordant choir.
- Because who knows the stripe of spirit raised by chains of paper dolls or what harm such idols constitute?
- Because this is not the day for shredding, for scraps, not the day for pieces, parts, or dross, not the day for wreckage – not even clipping stray threads from the best serge suit.

Sestina for Early Morning at the Service Station Coffee Shop

Six a.m. and the intersection lights flash
the end of night at an imperturbable rate,
a bloodless pulse reflecting a spilt-red glow
on the rained-on road. The sky, a tankish grey,
is cut with power lines scoring the morning,
a staff waiting for the music of destinations.

Customers, intent on their destinations,
arrive with the sun aiming its first flash
of light on surfaces. Clerks working the morning
shift flip switches and timers, prepare to rate
the chances of the day's success. The grey
appliances begin to hum to the pilot light's glow.

A heavy fridge door thuds. Outside, the glow
of headlights weakens as though the destinations
of vehicles are sure, as though the night's grey
residue is done. Something begins – a flash
of freshness, new coinage, at any rate,
new sounds, a new choir and mass for morning.

The silhouetted starlings wait for more morning –
they are not yet themselves. They know that DayGlo
signage will illuminate the first top-rate
feast of the day. Their preferred destination
is the parking lot where foil wrappings flash
amid the refuse sitting succulent and grey.

RALPH'S MOVING van arrives, its metallic grey
sides heaving at the drive-through for morning
coffee – dew-beads and their reflections flash
an eagerness, an expectation, a glow
that says something has lasted, that destinations
matter – can be reached – that moving vans rate.

The marvel of old beginnings – and the rate
of their return – steady, heedless of the grey-
hound in the pickup truck, nosing destinations,
breathless for things astir, keen to the morning
in his discerning way, welcoming the day's first glow –
and, tailgate down, ready to run in a flash.

No way to rate this clarity and the flash
of newness on all things old and grey, the glow
upon this destination, this station of the morning.

The Studio Boy's Private View
after a painting by Robert Harris, 1886 (Confederation Centre Art Gallery)

The Master's out for another tube of titanium white –
no palette knife or brush work yet on the canvas sketch –
but she's clearly here, her charcoal lines a presence
in the forming, outline enough to give a young man pause –
attendant to the Muse.

Portraiture may be the last thing on his mind,
in this, his brief respite from scuttle work and stoking coal.
No sable brush for him, his unassuming hands more deft
with corn-broom strokes across a smudgy floor,
sweeping out the atelier.

Still, keeping the motes of dust and soot at bay,
he plays his part, taking a breather, in the sitter's
figuring forth, her coming into being. Over-the-shoulder light
bestows its genius in the room, and now,
his gaze creates. He colours her.

But how shall he compose the rectangles of his life?
Diagonally? Must vision always be this chiaroscuro,
or might there be a landscape window-leap into a wilderness
of space? Something flowing or soaring beyond a boundary,
some uncomposed adventuring.

For the moment, though, he rests on a wicker seat
rapt by craft and baffled by the artistry of love –
and yet – yet, see how he's all fleshed out and suited up
in velvet trousers, blue-black vest, and homespun shirt,
clothed for work – for life. Already framed and hung,
yes, he so much more realized, so much more real than she.

Night Vision: Road Trip

I've driven down this road before – a thousand times.
Tonight, somehow, the road-feel of the car goes soft.
It's not the sidling moon ogling like a friendly fool –
no, what I'm losing are the speed lines, the racing stripes
peeling off my slick red fenders. The entire trip
slows down, and the headlamps sweep
over all passing things like searchlights at a border.
The double lines and dashes arrive as code
beyond deciphering, their only message: urgency.
Yellow diamonds make a slow approach, then flick
themselves incautiously into the dark behind my back.
Black-humped arrows, trapezoids, radiant circles,
woeful crosses, and oddly numbered junctions –
all routes, even the detours, are fateful.
There are strange readings on the instruments,
and the maximums are out of kilter – upper limits
on the pulse, say, or on days, or on an unknown quotient
explaining exclusions or what lies in between
what can be seen. Some kind of factoring is at hand.
A silhouetted boy and girl on their way to school
stride into view – holding hands with Memory,
should I brake for the past? Utility poles and shadowy trees
all strung together – the night-story a buzz of wires.
To the right, a laneway's red reflectors flash
like bloodshot eyes, while further on, just before MOTEL,
two more eyes shoot darts of light,
and a hobbling form drags itself into a ditch –
some animal, no doubt, cruising for flesh –
and next, a cattle-crossing to the other pasture
or God-knows-where. Hard to say.
Is this the signage to a terminus –
or just a garbled language stuttered by the dark?

Early Morning Mist

A soft breath has come to earth.
It must have paused a moment before
lowering its gentle weight upon the autumn fields,
before consenting to be contoured by the hills.
Now a muffled animal, it settles down
and spreads itself across the stubble,
threads its way among the lower branches of the spruce,
and brushes its back against the alder grove.
It weaves a shy course through the cattails
and strokes its cool palm over the hushed pond.

Its beauty comes from what it is –
unconcocted and easeful in its being;
neither rising nor falling, it takes the light
and comes or goes according to the way things are.
It bends its form to the world's shape.

Here, for this morning, this day,
a presence not meant to stay.

Not One Thing

That linden tree, the one by the shingled shed,
is not always the tree we take it to be,
shade for picnic table, pole for laundry line.
It is other than its bloom, its branch, and leaf,
its trunk not just a pillar, its bark not just a skin.
Not one thing. At times, unrooted,
it is something other than a tree,
an orb-like flower, bird-holder, leaf-clump,
child-machine – or a thing dissimilar,
a shoe, for instance, or a plate.
Fluttering with possibility, it goes beyond itself,
more than walking stick, guitar, or altarpiece,
even when it's leafless and winded by stirring words.
What it is, is quite other than its name,
its corrugated wrapping, its leopard spots,
and the twisting of its roads – really, it is original.
When rained upon, of course,
or ruffled in the fall, or frosted furry white,
one wonders – considering such unreliability –
that we tolerate its being in this world at all.

Once in a Lifetime

Once in a lifetime, perhaps, on a quiet,
almost breezeless night, when the rippling
of the river cracks the moon and sends
its shards downstream, one hears a blip
in the night's seamlessness –
a kind of slit in the surface of things,
as though something were leaving its world
and testing the waters, so to speak, of another.
Not every strolling couple or breathless runner
along the shore-side park has heard.
The fisherman, though, walking on
the granite wall drags his line in the dark,
trying hard, hoping for some kind of strike
before he reaches home. Behind him, the river
sutures the pale skin of each reflection
that he cuts.
                Further down, suspension cables
sling a bridge from shore to shore for trucks
that clank their way across the metal joints;
rivet by rivet, girders crisscross
themselves into a span. And then – beneath
its reach a search boat comes, bouncing its prow
and sweeping its cold blue light over every face.

Provisional

The marsh-hawk dives like there's no tomorrow,
and the starling's route from bush to vine
is a blur of moments, each one a *now*.
It gathers sticks and straw like a thing possessed,
As though that were it – that were the final nest.
The peony unfolds its lusciousness
without a thought to second tries;
the birch bud is eager – not shy.
And while the patient spider rests upon
what it has spun, it has confidence
that every filament is strung from twig
to stem with artful, perfect calibration.
In spring, the lean linden's only scaffolding
is shoot and leaf, the yearning branching built
to be its own sleek self. When tossed upon
the wind's conveyance, it sways knowing
that the storm's approach has no abeyance.

As kingfishers catch fire, dragonflies draw flame....

Gerard Manley Hopkins, "As Kingfishers Catch Fire"

Queen Anne's Lace
Daucus carota

One has to admire the nonchalance of your bloom,
white crown flung to the sun, swaying in a summer breeze,
your lah-lah-lah giddiness, lolling by the oat field.
Such pretension for a ditch weed, such finery among the
                                            verge dwellers –
dusty vetch, sow thistle, fleabane, and gaudy goldenrod –
lavish elegance holding roadside court,
umbel sophistication adorning a cow pasture.

Were it not for the florets' purple smudge,
we might pass by unaware of your pedigree.
As it is, that blush reminds us of the sovereign in her sewing room,
finger pricked, bestowing noble blood upon her handiwork –
tatting, perhaps, one more collar for a throne-room gown.

And now, on the margins, this decree:
common beauty stained with royalty.

Bestiary

Unnerving: that crow perched upon my roof,
staring me down, its bull neck
arched like a Tang-dynasty horse,

its beak aimed at all
my household carrion –
big bear of a bird, retching out

its caws, talons clutching
the rain-gutter, mulishly balking
at any adjustments to its *weltanschauung*.

And I, with beer in hand,
chaise longue by the patio table, lord it over
lawn and lake and barbeque deck,

smoke rising like an offering –
fat-spit and sizzle.
High-noon: the sun blinks, flares,

aims its light at my eyes;
a tinkling sound and a shower of sequins
falls gently over the clover.

The crow grows stick-like arms,
with little dark-feathered hands gripping
the asphalt shingles. It squawks and hisses.

Through my amber ale I see
the sleeping cat, limp and fat
by the fallen blossoms of the false spirea.

My limbs are brittle, tense, and oddly jointed;
Even the offshore breeze cannot stir
me in my birch-tree bower.

Elbows all akimbo at awkward angles,
I shuffle in the chair, feathers ruffled,
in need of equipoise, searching for ease.

Webworm

Hyphantria cunea

No Monarch you, pleb of the humble birch,
dull parasite of summer's green largesse,
lowly moth, destroyer who dares besmirch
my garden's spotless linden leafiness.
Unlessoned by the spider's dainty ruse,
you are all common worm and squirming sin,
spotted larvae, ravaging the elm whose
leaves you chew within the net you spin.
With little patterning and less design,
no silk from you, wayward weaver – no, just
a cloudy trap for currant bush, a shrine
to appetite that summons up disgust.
No wonder at the sight of you I'm cowed –
such interment, your foul late-summer shroud.

Paradisaea apoda

Linnaeus was in reality a poet who happened to become a naturalist.
– August Strindberg

Linnaeus thought you legless; thus,
your destiny was flight, restless flight
skimming the forest canopy –
no knowledge of the cool leaf
or clutched branch, remote
from eucalypt and sandalwood.

Your name spread like news of miracles –
crow-cousin, dew-drinker,
manuk dewata, God's own bird –
and Wallace, among natives,
bartered beads for word of you.
Passeros de col, avis paradiseus
bird of the sun, paradise bird.

Nothing but air and endless arcing
on a sultry breeze, or riding
the Warm Braw of a monsoon shore,
searching for the perfect glide,
anything for updraft ease –
all swoop and swerve,
your only stillness a stall before diving.

For some, mere sight of you
made fortune fat. Your golden feathers –
tokens of the afterlife – plucked
to top a lady's hat became
a nest of lavishness for drawing rooms.
Others, though, who glimpsed the blurry
sign of your high colour –
merciful bird – knew bestowal
of imaginings of rare design,
transporting thought, and iridescent speech.

It was death, of course, for those
who dared to craft the snares
that brought you down to earth.

For the Humpback Whales
Part One

I

Call me big wing –
I am *Megaptera*, the largest bird.
I have sea wings and fly with ease
over underwater mountains.
I sail above the sandy plain and skirt
the coastal reef with one stroke of my tail.
Bottom-feeders fear my shadow;
herring head for the hills, capelin for canyons.
I am sometimes very like a cloud,
for I eclipse the rays of upper light for hours
and hang in the sea's sky for days.

II

Since the Eocene my tail has penned
a cursive swirl across the waters of the earth.
My chronicle is longer than history,
longer than the fearsome stories of your imagination.
I go back before the monsters – before Leviathan.
I write of time, and the sea closes over it.
I write a water script from pole to pole.

III

I am Kaneloa – god of ocean animals.
I am beauty on a massive scale.
I am size and bulk and weight.
I expand and I displace.
My body is a fractal for the universe –
my largeness replicates its magnitude.
My splash repeats its rush
to occupy more and more space.
My shape, like certain moons, is perfectly aligned,
and my curvatures know endless amplitude.

IV

I breathe your air.
I, too, once slithered there among the fronds
in noisy fens with prickly plants
and squawks and furry things –
scarcely a memory now. Here,
I occupy the planet's greatest fluency.
Still, I break the sea's boundary,
give you back geysers of my breath,
and to your element make an offering
of my arching back, my fins, my gorgeous flukes.
I take what I need and leave you
the spectacle of my breach and fall –
the exploding flower of my stellar splash.
The slap of my fin is my parting shot.

V

I give the sea its name – whale road.
My road, my routes. In winter,
I circle in the warm Bermuda swells
until the Arctic calls. Northwards, then,
I map the contours of the continent
by Nantucket and Cape Cod,
by the Grand Banks of Newfoundland,
direct to the feasting grounds of Baffin Bay.
I am a dark needle magnetized by the high north.
I glide by my opposites, broken bergs,
bulks of icy whiteness drifting south – misshapen
North Atlantic ghosts provoking wonderment.

Part Two

VI

I ply all seas:
from the Moluccas and the Philippines,
past Kyushu and Honshu
to Kamchatka and the Bering Sea,
from the Azores to the Greenland Sea,
from Hawaii to Alaska's Gulf,
from Madagascar to the Persian Gulf.
And from the Weddell Sea at summer's end
I leave the krill-cold Antarctica,
round the Horn, then ride the Humboldt current,
and scale the Chilean Rise.
I trace the coastal trench past Peru and Ecuador,
northwards, where I mate
then loll in the warm Galapagos stream.

VII

With my spyhopping snout
in the air, my eye scouts the upper space.
I scan the choppy surf and accept
the homage of the jittery gulls.
I am the merry whale, the ocean's acrobat.
My breach is a leap into the next world,
my mighty crash, a welcoming return,
and my lob-tail slap and splash
an affirmation that I belong to both.

VIII

I am the singing whale –
Caruso of the deep, troubadour of the sea.
For many, many days, down the continental shelf,
I croon and bleat and moan.
For four thousand miles
my lyrics bounce from coast to coast,
eerie bleeps that echo through the depths
along the grand ledges of underwater stone.

IX

From cliffs on Ikitsuki Island, the temple monks
sing requiems and make their offerings –
they chant sutras for my dead.
For fifty million years I have coursed
the planet's seas – each arching of my back
a surfacing for you to wonder at.
Below, the sea anemones wave their tentacles
and shape their pulsing mouths to gaping O's.

X

On certain starlit nights,
when Cetus comes into the autumn sky,
grey-skinned islands have been known
to slide well out of sight – you may hear
the gulp and swish of their leeward glide.
Or, in the twilight of a breathless day,
where the shore-thrown foam and empty shells
meet the flat expanse of sea –
you may learn my oldest song:
hear me, hear me, hear me.

Lake Massawipi

Absurd, the snow-capped furniture upon the lawn –
blue jays know it, mocking the tilting table
by the well-windowed porch that sets its sights
upon a lake narrowing between the pines

but determined to go on, prairie of ice and snow
spread from shore to shore, delivering a silence
to the hibernating houses. No summer shouts –
even the echoes have been frozen mute.

Still, there are invitations here downwind,
as though its move to wilderness will speak
some kind of wisdom never heard on shore,
screened by fretwork of icy branches, filigree

of oak leaves, browned by the season, still shaking
in wisps of wind – cold jewellery of the year
rattling its disquiet. Some animal has braved
the lower inlet, left tracks, a trail – direct and purposeful.

But the sky is saying nothing, even though
the hills slope down to prod the lake to speech.
Nothing. Yet deep beneath the whiteness
a sapphire word is waiting to spread itself –

a sub-surface hope searching for the first slit in ice,
a motor boat etching its wake, a child's scream
from the diving raft. Something. One way or another,
whatever the season, we plunge into it.

Drift

Sky-stuff has come to meet the earth-force, this drift of snow
landing softly on the leaf-packed perennial bed by the garden shed.
Wind-driven from the west, it has skirted the shore-side cliff
and tunneled its torch of air through the back-field woods,
and then downhill, arced a cool weld across sheet-metal ice on the north-side
                                                                                                            lawn.
Leveled by its juncture with the hawthorn shrub, it birthed a curve
on the lee-drop of the poplar grove under whose shade it stretched a blue sinew
away from obstacles, its ridges marking boundaries, its planes intent on elegance.
This is the edge of something not quite known, the stroke of something cold,
a palette-knife swipe to paint the physics of the day, a commemoration of sorts,
an embodiment for sure – of the truth that cold destinations can be reached.
And now here it is, meandering to a white stillness, crystal by crystal,
though pressured by the wind – lift and down-draft contending for position.
Its white dust-up of metaphor puzzles a lone crow atop the swaying spruce.

The pain you feel is the pain of the outward, she said.
Later I will teach you the other pain.
When you have learned that you will be ready
to breathe fire.

– Patrick Lane, "The Firebreather"

The Brazen Bull

His screams will come to you through the pipes as the tenderest, most pathetic, most melodious of bellowings.

– Lucian, "The Bull of Phalaris"

Perillos to Phalaris: "more metalwork
than art, but the bronze has been beaten well.
Its flanks are strong and will draw the flames –
your victims' cries within will liven it."

Ingenious. Making death make music –
toneless death singing its own requiem.
He ought to have known that every artist
suffers for his work. Blame the anti-muse.

Ingenious. Tubing coiled at the mouth,
a rude horn bellowing out his fate,
oregano and thyme tossed in to mask
the roasting flesh. Spare the banqueters.

Throw the thing into the sea? Too late now.
Once realized, this is inspiration
for the ages. Precedent for agonies
and torturers is not so easily drowned.

That might explain our own Hereford bull
taking his mass to the far field
and braying out to sea – his sides heaving
rhythmically in the mist-enshrouded land.

From out his nostrils jets of bawling breath –
calling or keening? Who could know the nature
of such grief or suffering? Or was it bafflement
that he exhaled into the November air?

The Dictator's Son

Early memories? A child on the balcony, I saw cheering crowds
through the balustrades. I loved the buzz, and people's heads
were like the tops of spent blooms, a field of autumn flowers.
My toys echoed loudly through the palace corridors –
rat-a-tat-tat down the marble floors.

I waved my sticks and swords like a wand
over rows of noisy boots, coloured the fin-tailed missiles lavish pink –
made them into pretty fish. I was moved by the tank's tapered gun
raised like an arm; I learned to love the miles and miles
of upturned faces and the hail of *heils*.

I didn't plan it quite this way, but now it seems just right –
I know how to work a room, know when to stare, taking a bead
on my advisor's eye. Martial music stirs my blood – something about
percussive beats and four-four time. But, please, no epaulets or braid –
I prefer Armani, shapely cut with a touch of suede.

I do not presume. Still – my presence in a room has some effect,
I know how to make a scene, when to launch a rage,
and when to hush things down – tousle the child's glossy hair.
I've noticed that the handles of things fit well in my fist;
I know when to relent and when to twist.

A songbird's broken wing can make me weep,
and my taste in art is, well, conventional: shadowy folds of drapery
in an adoration or a Botticelli gown – that kind of thing.
True, Father's blockish statuary is destined to be mine,
but luckily, we agree on Brutalist for civic design.

No, I do not presume, but I prefer the lobby cleared
before my passing through. Yes, I know about the bunker rooms
with fetid smells and broken flesh; I *try* to use them sparingly –
really, I have little taste for concrete walls and splotchy stains,
for murky fluids swirling down dirty drains.

Porsche – the word is softness wrapping power,
though as for pleasure, I use my limousine to cruise
the market place – sometimes, spying her by a baker's stall.
Invitations to my rooms are rarely refused,
the pleadings in the half-light never excused.

Father's temper hardens like a gnarly root, and yesterday he tripped
upon a plaza stone. The gardeners keep a careful watch,
while I spend time turning over our accounts. Thankfully,
my infant neck escaped the jealous sword,
and Father, praise God, eschewed the strangler's silken cord.

Lone Wolf

In my brain, the pack remains –
the smell of so much rank fur.
We ran as one. Now I am the one –
I run alone.
Here at the forest's edge, snow in the clearing
is of little use to me. Day-stars in its crust
shine cold and hard – crystals sharp as claws.
The trees speak a foreign tongue,
a sub-zero cracking whose syllables
mean what I choose.
The brush of branch in the evening breeze
softens nothing,
and the beauty of blue shadows angers me.
I summon wrath at will.
On my way to the marshy pond,
where live things gather, I allow the dead weeds
to stroke my flanks.
It's worth it.
The snowdrift rat demeans my hunt,
and downwind comes the dirty scent of stag.
It soils my whitest field,
but I remember well the spray of red on snow,
a taste like no other.
It coils and coils itself into a core –
some shapeless thing whose birth
comes only with the dumb thud of smoke
and shrapnel showering the cratered earth.

Flowers by the Gates

Flowers by the gates of the fallen do not console.
Such proffering cannot contend with the stink
of their wilting, their mould, and the cellophane wrap
crinkling in the dirty old wind –

nor, just beyond the yellow tape strangling
the newly built Cape Cod, do the plastic eyes
and stitched smiles of plush toy bears. They sit drunkenly
among the weeds and unmowed grass.

Balloon bouquets festoon the broken fence,
while a chalked silhouette lies spread-eagled
with disjointed limbs like a muddied leaf
pressed upon the page of asphalt street.

Skid marks draw a tangent past them all,
past the rain-soaked verses and the mock chrysanthemums,
past the sputtering roses, and the pastel ribbons blowing
like a ragged flag – covenants from dollar stores.

Bone-white crosses hung with plastic wreathes
puzzle the fearful deer who sniff the greenery
by highway ditches – votive pits for invocations
and the tacky craft of memory turned memorial.

Meanwhile, the woeful semis sing lamentations
on their way to warehouse docks in foreign towns –
the freeway keen and requiem of eighteen-wheelers,
the mournful whine of many, many tires.

Elegy for Mikhail Kalashnikov
(1919 - 2013)

Tinkering with the recoil is one thing,
but 100 million AK 47s later
(many of them counterfeit), you have to wonder.

Had you been a poet – as you wished –
you could have scattered poems like air-dropped prayers –
warning shots.
Too late, now, to lament the farmers who will never see
your drafting table dreams – unrealized –
that superior potato tiller
or a better lawnmower for suburbanites.

Some legacies are lethal,
leaving collateral damage everywhere –
ragged edges around every wound.

Maybe you were better suited
to the machinery of metaphor
and the engineering of rapid-fire line-ends
grabbing attention amid the camouflage of words.

This is what comes of loading a gun,
latching in the magazines, with a rhyme scheme in mind.
Many modificatons later, you nailed it: pure poetry.

Little wonder you died humming the hymn of regret:
"The pain in my soul is unbearable."

Baumgartner's Fall
(from the edge of space October 14, 2012)

"It's all about coming home."
– Felix Baumgartner

Such egress at the edge
leaves us gasping for air,
desperate for your suit –
white as gull feathers,
sleek membrane between
upper spheres and frail bone.
Was that grace you slid through,
vast and thin, curvature
of clear blue light,
a mighty lens?
And beauty, too?
– a lingering, longing
look at the planet's
marbled swirl
and then
the necessary drop,
your Mach-one embrace
like a high priest
with arms outstretched blessing
the earth's dappled face.
That spin we've seen before,
blurry, tossed-down
angel
tumbling
into our
sleep,
troubling
the night's
equipoise.
The gliding, though,
was all joy beneath

the candy-coloured chute,
and such an easeful
end. But that's the thing
about descent:
it leaves a trace,
an echo, not the sound,
something remembered
but not quite known,
even while we kneel
thankful on the desert ground.

Lost with *The Titanic*: An Inventory

1
Merry-Joseph Blondel's *La Circassienne au Bain*

This is the loneliest art – sunken back to nature
at an ocean's remove, Circassian loveliness
in mountains never seen. North Atlantic irony:
amid the greenery, a woman dips her toes into a bath
filled from a spigot's stream – the marble walls
springing a leak. Her silken drapery curls about her form,
more revealing than concealing – and drifts
like seaweed among the dogfish and the mackerel.
Here in the murk, colour scarcely matters;
the pigments go obscure, and brilliance darkens under sand –
rose madder, umber, and ultramarine.
So much for sighs and smiles from drawing room
to dining room – so much for gilt and Fontainebleau décor.
Beauty at this depth requires another name – a word
mouthed by darkness under a vast line of pure white stars.

II

The Rubaiyat of Omar Kayyam translated by Edward Fitzgerald
(*"The Great Omar,"* eds. Sangorski and Sutcliffe: jewelled edition)

This proves his point – a thousand gems
disappear, losing lustre on the ocean's
floor. Blown roses scatter
beauty further than any facet here.

At depths like these, clock and compass
fail – sea grass, kelp, and wrack
swirl more gracefully than any
tooled vine or peacock tail.

Agreed – there's no erasing truths
one's life has written on the wall,
yet, creatures pause open-mouthed
to watch these soggy pages bleed.

Cold currents make a mockery
of thirst. When spilled like this, even
rare vintages are sobering – pleasure
spoiled, diluted, and thoroughly dispersed.

III

Five Grand Pianos

1.

My sounds were big left-handed chords,
descending decrescendo, rumbling down
to a darkened pianissimo –
to understatement, and then, beyond.
The smallest wave becomes submerged, subsumed –
silence flowing northward under bergs.

2.

My voice rang clear, sought light
and an upper sphere on an upwards scale,
the final treble note surfacing for air –
more imagined than real,
more gasp than breath,
more voiceless scream than song.

3.

I made the dancers dance.
I was all beat – ballroom waltz and up-tempo groove,
all red-blooded pulse and staccato finger snap.
It's a sad dance now – there's no embracing in the icy waves,
no tango with a heartless tide.
Rhythm breaks – the dancer freezes on the floor.

4.

I relished melody –
befriended memory.
Mouths mouthed me.
But now? Nothing
but a tuneless tone,
a nameless monotone,
unknown to any scale,
a tone to end all tones,
a tone without a song.

5.

I was made for harmony –
always enjoyed a crowd,
could manage a deft touch with dissonance.
Sonority was my second name.
My sum was always greater than my parts.
But now, I hear only
The Long Silent Note,
a muffled singleness that offends my ear
and remains unplayable on any of my keys.

An Architect Visits the Sick

How could he not fall in love with Japan, where in times past when someone became ill an architect was called in first, rather than a doctor?

– David Stourck, *Arthur Erickson: an Architect's Life*

His approach at the door, no doubt, was soft –
parting the *noren*, splitting the darkness,
steps like spots of light on a forest floor –
the prone body, a block of marble toppled
on its plinth. After the bowing,
questions about soundness of structure
and damage sustained by the elements.
His first suspicion? Sub-standard materials
for the body's post-and-beam.
Then, knuckling the buckled breast,
smoothing a hand over trunk and limb –
would there be measurements to calibrate proportions
and the use of space? How would hand-clap and bell-ring
restore the crumbling sill, the blistered wall, and rotted roof?

Doctor or priest? It amounts to the same –
each wondering what buttressing should be prescribed,
agreeing at the end that a waterfall was right –
and ample fenestration to allow more light from the bamboo grove.

THE NORTH RIVER FIRE HALL SUITE II

Think of yourself, almost a god,
Your hair on fire,

The bellows of your heart pumping.

– Mark Strand, "What to Think of"

THE WORST FIRE ESCAPE PLAN IS NO PLAN.

I

2:33 a.m.
and the red hot bedroom clock
brands the hour into the darkness of the room.
Shapes are slurred, and crackles
in the radiator are impossible to track –
something in the pipes is playing tricks.
Outside, animals awaken
and scamper up the downspout.
Thieves have jimmied the basement window
and are spilling gasoline.
Burners turned off?
Fireplace coals, spitting across the carpet,
ignite the fuse of draperies
and make a toxic cauldron of the livingroom.
Smoke walls up the exit.
Windows pop.

And so –
I will tie the bed sheets in Boy Scout knots,
chair-smash the bathroom window –
neighbours, huddled in their coats,
will cheer me on. I will shimmy down
to the lookout roof, zig-zag around
the falling cinders, Zorro-leap to catch
the largest linden branch and drop
to the lower balcony. From there,
it's a short leap down to the freshly turned
dahlia bed, which is sure to break my fall.

By then, flames will have licked the siding clean
and broken through the roof.
Everyone will marvel at the shapes of blackened things
left behind – bits of the past flaring for a moment
in a gusty northeast wind,
then vanishing in clouds of smoke darker than night.

**SHORT-CUTS IN LIFE
CUT LIFE SHORT.**

II

Well, sure. A hastily sharpened knife
draws blood. And who wants to cross
a bridge riveted with sub-standard steel?
Or brave an unlit alley? Or chance
the frozen river rather than go around?

But sometimes on our way to the shore,
we would leave the dusty road and cross
the hill field – never mind the barbed-
wire snagging; once freed, we aimed
our diagonal true, waded through
the windrows of newly mown hay, made
a bee-line over clover to the crumbling cliff.

Voices trailed behind us, faded –
shouts to bring the hammer, calls to pick
the berries – we made straight to the screak
of gulls testing the long thin sandbars
warmed by the summer sun; with beach-towel
wings, we lifted off the runways,
learned daring dives and underwater tricks,
lolled in the gullies, and splashed our way
through the afternoon. The hours flowed
like strands of purple kelp, floating
pliantly – unfolding easefully with every wave.

Surely – surely, the route we took to that,
added years to our lives.

FIREFIGHTERS SAVE HEARTS AND HOMES.

III

An Allegory

The first sign of a flue fire is a roaring from within –
a whomp and whoosh from the basement, a second flaming
up the spine of the house that takes you by surprise.
But make no mistake, it's been growing there for months.
Hours and hours of burning, sometimes hot and clean –
well-seasoned sticks of knotty oak will do that –
sometimes slow and smouldering – scraps of uncured spruce.

Either way, smoke cools and sticks to the red-brick walls.
Creosote preserves some flesh of every burning;
it is the blackening that grows, the tar that stays
after the body has been warmed by the reading chair,
after the kettle sings, after the aromatic tea, after the nodding
and all the wise words from the dropped book –
after the dog has stretched and sighed on the hearth-side rug.

What starts the fiery exhalation is unpredictable:
too much stoking, too much poker work,
a wayward nor'easter buffeting a twisty downdraft,
or the tinder of discarded wrappings from the Christmas celebrations.
Once ignited, though, the upwards torch is a force
to be reckoned with – flames igniting flame –
a whirlwind hot enough for prophets.

The only options are prayer and a curse –
perhaps, an invocation of lucky numbers.
The 9-1-1 rescue trucks, however, offer
no hard proof of release, even though the extinguishing
will leave a quiet sadness among all burnt desires –
at best what will remain is one revolving light
throwing its red warning over ashes and the gathering crowd.

ALWAYS LEAVE YOURSELF AN EMERGENCY EXIT.

IV

Yeah, right. Like the rear one
on a burning 747 in a spinning dive
aimed at the blue concrete of Baffin Bay.
Or the cellar stair splintering up
in the latest super-sonic Kansas twister.

Overhead, wild geese beat it south,
honking their ironic warning.

Sometimes, there is no walk-through corridor,
and alternatives are hardly that:
dropping a knee, outstretched arms.
At least, these days, there may be
a cell-phone photo of the drama –
one night's flash upon the news screen
(underneath the overprint of rebate offers
or scrolling across the lesser wars
coming in on a direct feed).

Ladders? Rickety, unreliable things
whose rungs disappear in the darkness
at either end.

See the cat skedaddle through the yard,
lean into a sudden swerve,
and disappear into the undergrowth.

Escape may be the membrane between
this room's fire and the next-door flood.
Still, it's nice to think that, as the music swells
and things deteriorate in the sodden light
of the hotel bar, one can always dash
for the door beneath the blood-red exit sign –
that metal clunk releasing you to backlot bins
and the sobering flare of a midday sun.

LUCK RUNS OUT, BUT SAFETY IS GOOD FOR LIFE.

V

Although –
the line between the two is sometimes snug,
the margin, safety-razor thin.
One slip of the wrist or a miscalculation
in direction and blood will leave
its fine brush stroke across the skin.

Safety catches?
Tell the grazing doe startled
by a click deep within the thicket.

Tell the fearful woman fumbling with the latch.
Luck follows her running into the street,
dish towel waving surrender to the lightning strike
that leaves the kitchen window
glowing smoky red.

Luck running out? Not mine.
I want my luck pinched at the waist, an hourglass
with that flip-it-over, begin-again drip of sand –
rock-crush, fallout from stars –
buff-coloured time in a do-over world.

Relics

First Class
(Bone, blood, or flesh)

After last night's storm –
wind-wrack and dismemberment –
broken branches lie disjointed everywhere,
marrow-dry but worth the gathering.
And the newest, greenest leaf
pressed between the pages of a book
will mark the stopping place –
a beautiful pause for thought,
for memory, and all wise words.
So, too, autumn's fallen leaf
from the dusty lane's ancestral tree
deserves its veneration – blown about
and caught beneath the boxwood hedge.
And bits of paper birch, speckled
white, flap raggedly – they warrant
the reverence towards a torn shroud.

Second Class
(Owned objects)

Surely, what lodged within your
branches just out of sight
belonged to you, for a time at least –
the robin's nest and its turquoise eggs.
These, too, deserve the adoration
of cradling in cupped hands.
The farmer's coat hung upon
the lowest limb, the garden tools
leant against your trunk,
the cooling shade – all these
bespoke your placement in the world.
As for the remnant strings
of kites snarled there all
summer long, such tatters
prove the wholeness of your form,
a matchless crown of leafy loftiness.

Third Class
(Objects touched)

Your rustling was a cool beneficence
on hot summer nights – the bay-side
breeze entered you, flowed through you,
divided and subdivided its blessings.
Even the dark jagged shapes
flitting by like spirits on the prowl –
the ones we could not name –
they, too, knew the ins and outs
of that great bowl of greenery.
And then, each night a miracle –
the good works of your branches
summoning the moonrise, its
blood-orange light reflected in the bay –
a radiance upon you, slantwise,
while your midnight shadows
placed soothing hands upon the field.

NOTES

1. (page 10) "A spark neglected makes a mighty fire." Robert Herrick, "Another," No. 875. *Hesperides*.

2. (page 27) "A Concert at Chapelle Notre-Dame-de-Bon-Secours." Following a tradition begun in 1840, authorities of the Port of Montreal award The Gold-Headed Cane to the captain of an ocean-going vessel that first reaches Montreal in the New Year.

3. (page 38)
   Robert Harris (1849-1919)
   The Studio Boy's Private View, 1886
   oil on canvas
   89.5 x 74.5 cm
   Gift of an anonymous donor, 1978
   Collection of the Confederation Centre Art Gallery, CAG H-571

4. (page 45) "Queen Anne's Lace." According to legend, the red or purple colour at the centre of some flowers of this plant represents a spot of blood spilled when Queen Anne pricked her finger making lace. The legend may refer either to Queen Anne (1574–1619), the first Stuart Queen married to James of Scotland or to Queen Anne (1665–1714), the daughter of William and Mary.

5. (page 48) "*Paradiseae apoda*" (or "legless bird-of-paradise"). Carl Linnaeus (1707–78) so named the Indonesian species because he thought it legless owing to European trade in these stuffed birds with legs removed. Alfred Russell Wallace (1823-1913), a British naturalist, spent six years in the Malay archipelago collecting species, including the *paradiseae apoda*.

6. (page 63) "Baumgartner's Fall." On October 14, 2012, from a capsule lifted by a helium balloon to a height of 38, 969.4 m, Felix Baumgartner successfully freefell and parachuted from "the edge of space." In the process, he broke the sound barrier.

ACKNOWLEDGEMENTS

"For the Humpback Whales" was commissioned by
Carnegie Hall for a concert program, "Voice of the Whale,"
performed May 17, 2009 in New York at the American
Museum of Natural History by Ensemble ACJW, fellows of
The Academy, a joint program of Carnegie Hall,
The Juilliard School, and the Weill Music Institute.
Co-readers of the poem were the author and Fabien Cousteau.

"Not One Thing" was a finalist in the 2013 *Malahat Review*
annual poetry competition.

"Bestiary" first appeared in *The Malahat Review*
(No. 180, Autumn 2012).

The manuscript benefited immeasurably from the
keen editorial eye and judicious advice of Anne Compton.
Special thanks are also extended to Kay Diviney and John Smith.
A poet could find no better "first responders" who rescued
many of these poems from their perilous early drafts.